copyright © 2018 Cantemos all rights reserved

All photographs are the property of Ishrani Annamunthodoo and may not be copied, reproduced or used in any manner without the written consent of the photographer.

On the cover a RED NECK GREBE chick

Cantemos Tel. 909-239-2735

http://www.cantemosco.com

bakergeorgette@yahoo.com

Introduce a child to bird watching with this colorful array of photographs. Teach the name, look for the bird, repeat the rhyme. Buy wild bird food and put it out to observe birds where you live. Enjoy!

Georgette

Bird Book for Kids

Observando Aves

by Georgette Baker

Photographs by Ishrani Annamunthodoo

What bird is that? The one I can see.

¿Que pájaro es ese? El que veo allí.

That is an **OYSTER CATCHER** someone told me.

Es un **OSTRERO** me dijeron a mi.

What bird is that? The one in the tree.

Que pájaro es ese? En el árbol allí.

That is a EASTERN BLUE BIRD someone told me.

Es un AZULEJO ORIENTAL me dijeron a mi.

What bird is that? The one I can see.

That is a ROAD RUNNER someone told me.

¿Que pájaro es ese? El que veo allí.

Es un CORRECAMINOS me dijeron a mi.

What bird is that, with the really long tail?
That is a LONG TAILED DUCK, he is a male.

¿Que pájaro es ese con la cola larga?
Es un PATO DE COLA LARGA.

The GREAT EGRET preens.

La GRAN GARCETA arregla sus plumas con el pico.

The GREAT EGRET flies.

La GRAN GARCETA vuela.

The TERN found food.

A YELLOW RUMPED WARBLER found food.

The SONG SPARROW found food.

Todos estos pájaros encontraron comida.

The OSPREY found food.

The male HOODED MERGANSER found food.

The GROUND OWL lives in holes in the ground.

EL BUO HABANERO vive en huecos en la tierra.

These are ducks, they love water. They have webbed feet.

REDHEAD DUCK

PATO PELIROJO

WOOD DUCK , male

PATO JOYUYO, macho

D NECK GREBE

MORMUJO CUELLIRROJO

stos son patos, les gustan el agua. Tienen patas palmeadas.

Two BLACK-NECKED STILTS

Dos ZANCOS DE CUELLO NEGRO

ne SPOTTED TOWHEE.

n RASCADOR

Two PIGEONS

Dos PALOMAS

EAGLE

Bird

AGUILA

OSPREY

AGUILA PESCADORA

GREAT HORNED OWL

GRAN BUHO

BLACK CAPPE
CHICKADEE

CARBONERO

LESSER
GOLDFINCH

JILGUERO

BLUE JAY
QUERRE-QUERRE

TUFTED TITMOUSE
CERRILLO BICOLOR

HOUSE FINCH   PINZON

FEMALE
HEMBRA

MALE
MACHO

WHITE CROWNED SPARROW

GORRION CORONADO BLANCO

VERMILLION FLYCATCHER

MOSQUERO BERMELLON

LADDERBACK WOODPECKER

PAJARO CARPINTERO

GREEN HERON

GARZA VERDE

What bird is that? The one I can see.
That is a COMMON GRACKLE someone told me.

¿Que pájaro es ese? El que veo allí.

Es un ZANATE COMUN me dijeron a mi.

INTERESTING FACTS

rds of prey have talons to catch and
ld their prey.

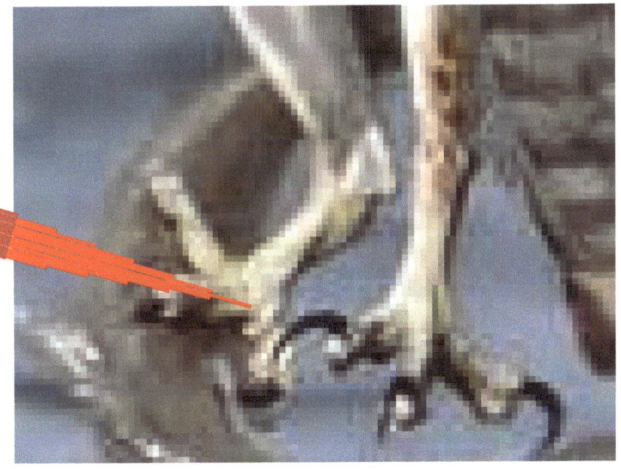

s aves de rapiña tienen
rras para coger y sujetar sus pre-

cks can be found in freshwater and saltwater.

s patos pueden ser encontrados en agua dulce y sal-

geons are related to the DODO which is now extinct .

lomas están relacionadas a LA DODO que está ahora extinto.

e most common bird in the world is the HOUSE SPARROW.

 ave más común en el mundo es el GORRIÓN.

www.ingramcontent.com/pod-product-compliance
Lightning Source LLC
Chambersburg PA
CBHW041503220426
43661CB00016B/1235